W9-BFU-165

STILL MISSING BEULAH
Stories of Blacks and Jews
in Mid-Century Miami

Joan Lipinsky Cochran

Perricot
Publishing

This is a work of fiction. All of the characters, organizations and events in this novel are either products of the author's imagination or are used fictitiously.

www.joanlipinskycochran.com.
Published by Perricot Publishing
Book cover design by Jennifer Musselman
First printing

ISBN-13: 978-0-6922-9835-0
ISBN-10: 0-6922-9835-5

To my parents
Helaine and Murray Lipinsky

Table of Contents

Introduction

I was a young reporter fresh out of journalism school in the spring of 1975, manning the city desk of the now-defunct *Hollywood Sun-Tattler*, when an anonymous call came in. The Ku Klux Klan was trying to march in a Boy Scout parade in Davie. Would I send someone to cover it? I was stumped. I wasn't supposed to leave the office and was afraid to call the city editor, a man with an explosive temper who'd berate me for calling him on Sunday morning.

I grew up in Miami and, until high school, hadn't given much thought to the "coloreds only" drinking fountains and rest rooms along Florida's turnpike or the fact that only a few of my classmates were black. That's the way things were. But by this point in my life, I was appalled by the Klan and all they symbolized— for Jews and blacks. I *had* to call my city editor. He harangued me for bothering him. But, to his credit, he decided the bigots didn't deserve our coverage.

Black and Jewish relations in Miami have long intrigued me, in part because both groups have been marginalized from the earliest days of South Florida history. Before World War II, Jews were rarely allowed to stay in hotels north of Fifth Street in Miami Beach.

As recently as the 1970s, country clubs had gentlemen's agreements to keep "Hebrews" out. The situation was far worse for African Americans, who were subject to the same indignities in purportedly liberal South Florida they faced in the heart of Dixie. Black people, including entertainers as renowned as B.B. King and Nat King Cole, were forbidden to stay on Miami Beach at night. African Americans in Miami were banned from "whites only" beaches and restaurants.

This linked short story collection explores the complex relationships between Miami Jews and blacks through the eyes of a cantankerous elderly Jewish man and the daughter he raised in Miami during the 1950s and 1960s. Each short story is followed by a brief account of a racially-related or anti-Semitic event that occurred in South Florida and that illuminates the era in which the story takes place.

When reading these stories and historic accounts, I hope you become lost in Tootsie and Rebecca Plotnik's world—a world that existed long before Miami became the gateway to the Americas, and before Spanish and Creole became as common as English in its streets and schools. I also hope you walk away with a sense of the events, people and settings that made mid-century Miami unique as the most culturally "northern" and liberal of Florida's cities while retaining some of the most deplorable characteristics of America's Deep South.

Joan Lipinsky Cochran
September 2014

Still Missing Beulah

My eyes dart from the gold-rimmed plate on my father's lap to the white brocade couch on which the old man sits. He just returned from the buffet table in Fannie Farbish's dining room, where he helped himself to a generous serving of creamed herring and onions, a garlic bagel and a slab of beef tongue slathered with bright yellow mustard.

I cringe as he lifts his right thigh to cross his legs. At eighty-six, he's none too steady and has, I'm betting, a fifty-fifty chance of dumping his food on the couch. Elbows raised in a birdlike wingspan, he grasps the edges of the plate between his thumbs and forefingers and mounts one thigh over the other. When he returns the plate to his lap, I release my breath. My father is *not* going to create a greasy schmear on Fannie Farbish's immaculate white sofa.

Not that Fanny Farbish would mind. In point of fact, she's been dead for three days. The old lady, my father explained on the drive over, has been circling the drain for the last year. So her demise did not come as a complete surprise. Dr. Farbish, Fannie's devoted husband of fifty-three years, had plenty of time to make arrangements before his wife passed on.

I have not been inside the Farbish home in forty years and am surprised to find it unchanged since the days when I'd stop by on my way home from school to visit our housekeeper, Beulah. A lanky black woman, she cleaned three times a week for my family and twice a week for Mrs. Farbish. Every Tuesday and Thursday, on Mrs. Farbish's days, I'd ring the Farbish's doorbell, confident that Beulah would be there to envelop me in a big hug and the comforting scents of pine cleaner and starched cotton. Mrs. Farbish napped in the afternoon, which left us free to talk. While Beulah prepared Dr. and Mrs. Farbish's dinner, I'd tell her about my latest argument with my best friend, Augie, which boy I had a crush on that week and, especially in the last months of our visits, the agonizing tedium of memorizing lines of Hebrew for my bat mitzvah.

Standing in the Farbish dining room a few minutes earlier, I'd experienced a vertiginous sense of déjà vu. Brightly-painted Peter Max prints still filled the entire west wall of the dining room and the oversized art books on the glass and chrome buffet remained where Mrs. Farbish placed them in the 1970s. As I glanced into the kitchen on my way to the living room, I imagined Beulah standing in front of the oven with her arms folded across her chest and the old familiar gap-toothed smile on her face. For the briefest moment, I inhaled the aroma of chicken deep frying in lard— Beulah's specialty.

"Darling, how are you?"

A familiar voice breaks into my reveries and I turn to find my mother's best friend, Edith, approaching from the dining room. As always, she is fastidiously dressed, though her pink silk suit hangs a bit too loosely

4

on her frame and she no longer wears spiked heels. Her long, brown curly hair has given way to a stiff silver fresh-from-the-beauty parlor pageboy and tastefully-modest diamond studs sparkle in her earlobes. Edith's smile, broad and welcoming, fades as she shifts her gaze to my father. I don't know whether to be amused or upset when she glares at him, then purses her lips in a moue of disgust.

"Tootsie," she says in a tone that welcomes no response. She gives a brisk nod, then turns back in the direction from which she's come.

"Why don't we visit in the kitchen, dear?"

"Looks like I'm still *persona non grata*," my dad—everyone calls him Tootsie—whispers, bringing his lips close to my ear. "Those old broads never forget, do they?"

As my mom's best friend, Edith knew about my dad's affairs. And while I'd long ago resolved to let go of my resentment toward the old man, I've grown accustomed—if not entirely comfortable—to listening to her old friends retell horror stories about him. Good gossip and a sense of righteousness don't seem to die when the victim of those sentiments passes on.

"I'd like to say hello. After I talk to Edith, we can head home," I say, patting the old man's shoulder. "That okay?"

He shrugs. "Knock yourself out."

I rise from the couch and enter the kitchen, where Edith's chatting with Selma, another friend of my mother. I know my dad's cheating is common knowledge, but wince as Selma relates a particularly sordid story about his affair with a "young" neighbor who must be in her seventies at this point. My mother's been gone five years now and I feel vaguely disloyal to my father for listening to these tales. But it seems to be the only thing I have in common with my mom's friends.

After promising Selma and Edith that I'll stay in touch, I head back to the living room and spot Tootsie coming toward me through the dining room. He looks dapper with his slim frame, expensively-tailored suit and shock of silvery-white hair and I'm jolted by the realization he's still attractive.

"You finished?" he says, meeting me in the door to the kitchen, "because I'm ready to get out of here."

"Aren't you going to offer your condolences to Dr. Farbish?"

"What for? He doesn't need it. Farbish can get on with his life now, find himself a hot, young babe."

"Dad!"

My father smirks.

I glance over his shoulder at Dr. Farbish, who stands at the foot of the dining room table. Small, rimless spectacles rest on his nose and his hands clasp an ample stomach. Sheila Sackowitz, Fannie's best friend, pats his arm as they speak.

"It's funny but the only thing I remember about Mrs. Farbish was how much I hated her after she stole Beulah," I whisper as we approach our host. "I never talked to her after that."

My dad raises an eyebrow but says nothing.

After offering Dr. Farbish our condolences, my father and I return to my car and back out of the driveway into the street we called home for thirty years. I reduce my speed as we pass my family's old house, five doors from the Farbish's. The latest owners have painted the front door bright red but left the stucco walls the same pale grey my mother chose forty years ago. The small oaks she planted in the front yard tower over the road.

"That business back there about Mrs. Farbish stealing Beulah. What did you mean?" Tootsie asks as we pull onto Ponce de Leon Boulevard.

"You remember. Just before my bat mitzvah, Beulah left to work for the Farbishes full time."

It's been almost forty years, but a familiar ache fills my chest. Beulah came to work for my family when I was three and I quickly became her shadow. As I got older, my mother teased me about following Beulah around with a rag, trying to help but—more often than not—getting in the way. She became the one person I could confide in when Esther, my older sister, was mean to me or my parents fought. When Beulah passed away ten years earlier, I started wearing the gold circle pin she gave me for my eighth birthday.

"Who told you Beulah left us for Mrs. Farbish?" my dad asks. "Your mother? Grandma Sadie?"

"Neither. Why else would she leave?" I look toward my father and realize my parents never discussed Beulah's departure. "Don't you remember? Just before my bat mitzvah when things were so bad. You and Mom fought every night. When Beulah came to work, she spent hours listening to Mom's problems. She had to stay late to get her work done."

"I don't remember that."

Of course not, I think. You were always out of town *on business*.

"When Mom told us Beulah wasn't coming back, I figured she got tired of the fighting and of Mom crying.

7

All Mom told me was that Beulah was working for Mrs. Farbish a few more days a week. I was sure Beulah would've come back if Mrs. Farbish hadn't hogged her time."

The old man shakes his head and rolls his eyes. It's an oddly adolescent gesture for an elderly man and reminds me of the derisive faces he made when my mother announced Grandma Sadie was coming for a visit.

I pull to the traffic light on Ponce and wait to turn onto Dixie Highway. It's green, but traffic is heavy for a Sunday night and it takes a moment for the intersection to clear.

We drive about two blocks before my father smacks the dashboard with his fist. I jump and glance over at him before returning my eyes to the road.

"It was the old lady. Your grandmother."

"What about her?"

"*She* got Beulah to leave."

I hit the brakes a bit too hard as I near the red light at Le Jeune. My father rocks forward and catches himself on the dash.

"Are you telling me Grandma fired Beulah?"

"Just about. Remember how attached you were to Beulah?"

"What about it?"

"Your grandmother had a problem with that."

"What kind of problem?"

"Who knows? All I know is the old yenta told Beulah the two of you were too close and that it interfered with your relationship with your mother."

"She didn't?"

"The old lady wouldn't shut up on the subject. I'd

catch her in the kitchen talking to Beulah and she'd clam up."

"You're telling me Beulah left because of Grandma?"

"Why would I make it up?

I laugh.

My father twists his lips then gives me a dirty look. "I didn't have much good to say about your Grandma Sadie, but I cared about Beulah." He turns to face me. "Ten years she was with us. Of course I was upset when she left. Your mother was devastated. I never told her it was because of the old yenta."

"Why are you so sure?" I'd never seen him speak to Beulah other than to thank her for finding his keys.

"A couple of days before the bat mitzvah, I think it was a Thursday, I left work early and stopped by the Farbishes. I knew Beulah would be there. She started crying when I came into the house, apologized for leaving. I teared up too. She practically raised you girls."

My throat grows dry as I clench the wheel. "What did she say? What *exactly* did she say?"

"For Christ sake, it's been forty years." He reaches over and redirects the air conditioning vent, blasting me with cold air. "Okay. Near as I can remember, Beulah said she was sorry you got so attached to her, that she realized she'd come between you and your mother. She said she didn't recognize what was happening until Grandma Sadie pointed it out. Beulah didn't feel she could, what is it, wean you off? She had to make a clean break and she didn't have the heart to tell you. And when Mrs. Farbish asked her to work the extra days, well, she took up the offer."

I continue driving, passing a gas station, an automotive parts store, then the Japanese restaurant I reviewed for a newspaper a week earlier. My palms feel damp on the wheel as I recall the weeks before my bat mitzvah.

What my father says makes sense. Grandma Sadie stayed with us to help my mom prepare some of the dishes served at my bat mitzvah reception. After all these years, I still recall how disappointed and heartbroken I was when my mother told me Beulah was not coming back. It was about a week before my big day and I refused to believe her. But I cried the morning of my bat mitzvah when it hit me that Beulah really and truly wouldn't share what felt like the most important day of my life.

The traffic eases as Dixie Highway merges into I-95 and, in fifteen minutes, I'm descending the Biscayne Boulevard off ramp and driving through the streets of downtown Miami. They're eerily deserted on a Sunday afternoon—the stores are shuttered and the panhandlers have taken their business elsewhere. The sky grew dark as I drove north and I scan the horizon for thunderheads. There are none. I check the clock on my dashboard and realize it's almost eight. I'd stayed at the Farbishes longer than I'd planned, which means returning to an empty house in the dark, one of the drawbacks of forcing my husband to move out. I pull to the front of my father's building—an independent living facility on the campus of the Schmuel Bernstein Jewish Home for the Aged—and leave the engine running.

"I visited Beulah, too, a week after my bat mitzvah," I say. My dad, who's reaching for the door handle, turns back to me, a quizzical expression creasing his eyes. "I begged her to come back. Told her I'd get you and mom to stop fighting. She said she still loved me and that I should take care of Mom. But she wasn't coming back and wouldn't tell me why."

My father nods slowly, rubbing his chin with his hand. "She was a good woman and didn't want you to resent your grandmother."

I laugh. Tootsie detested my Grandma Sadie and never missed a chance to criticize her. He'd hardly pass up the opportunity to blame her for Beulah leaving.

"So how did *you* keep it a secret?" I ask.

He shrugs, missing or ignoring the skepticism in my voice. "You and your mother were under a lot of pressure getting ready for your big day. I didn't want to ruin it for you." He looks at me out of the corner of his eye. "And then, I don't know, there didn't seem to be any point in letting either of you know. It would only hurt you."

My dad gets out of the car, but leaves the door open and leans in. "You know what I say. What's done is done. The old lady flew back to New York, and I went back to work to pay off your big party. Mom hired that cleaning girl, Marianna, and we were fine." He leans further into the car, reaches a hand across the seat and pats my cheek. "And Mrs. Farbish, may the old broad rest in peace, got the best deal of all."

I remain at the curb with my engine idling and watch Tootsie enter the building. The sliding glass doors whisk open to usher him back into the world of fluorescent lighting, black linoleum hallways, and metal walkers. It's a far cry from our old neighborhood with its sweeping lawns and noisy children. I wonder if my mother suspected that Grandma Sadie drove Beulah away. Or that my father asked her to return. I decide not. Sharing the truth would have meant confessing he'd done a kindness for my mother. And that was something he could never admit.

Not in My Eden Roc

In the 1940s, Miami Beach hotels boasted entertainment every bit as sizzling as that of Broadway and Las Vegas. Sammy Davis Jr., Nat King Cole, Harry Belafonte and Ella Fitzgerald were among the stars who performed at such glamorous hotels as The Eden Roc and Fontainebleau.

Despite their international fame, these black headliners were forbidden to stay in Miami Beach hotels. As with the African American maids and gardeners who made their way across Biscayne Bay to work on Miami Beach each morning, black entertainers had to return to Miami's "Colored Town" at night.

Many stayed in hotels on Second Avenue in the heart of the bustling neighborhood known as Overtown. While black people were forbidden on Miami Beach at night, whites could cross the bay and join them in clubs at the Mary Elizabeth Hotel and the Rockland Palace. There, all were welcome to watch the likes of Cab Calloway, Benny Goodman and B.B. King perform deep into the evening.

Integration and poorly-wrought urban planning brought an end to this historically-significant African American enclave. By the 1960s, people previously allowed to shop only in black areas were permitted in stores in downtown Miami. When state legislators voted to construct Interstate 95 through the heart of Overtown in the 1960s, they effectively rang the death knell for this culturally-rich African American district.

Tootsie's *Schvartze*

My father's full of piss and vinegar tonight. When I get to his apartment at the Schmuel Bernstein Jewish Home for the Aged, he's standing with the door open, squirming like a kid with a secret. I figure he's been sitting by the window for a half hour, watching for the so-called "classic" Mercedes my husband Harold left behind when I threw him out. Unlike his Volkswagen, which spends its life in the shop, the Mercedes Harold bought second hand twenty-five years ago refuses to die.

My father's been *hocking* me all week about the stuffed cabbage he scored at Epicure, a gourmet grocery across the causeway from the Schmuel Bernstein. Back in the fifties, when Miami Beach was a refuge for retired Jews, everyone went there for their borscht, chopped liver and matzo balls. Straight from the *shtetl*, the Old World, my father claims. The Epicure still caters to the old Jews. But they also stock gourmet cheeses and mineral water for the skinny models and what my father calls *feygelehs*—Yiddish slang for gay men.

Stuffed cabbage is a big deal for the old man. He asks me to make it at least once a month since my mom passed away. "No one," he insists, "makes stuffed cabbage like my Bernice. Hers was the best."

I can't argue with that. Earlier this week, when he called and asked me to make it, he acted like I was holding out. "A *baleboosteh* like you. A big shot food writer. You're running her *lukshen kugel* and chicken soup recipes in the newspaper. And you can't come up with her stuffed cabbage?"

Maybe he heard me shrug over the phone or tired of riding my rear. "Okay," he conceded, "Mildred Goldfarb's daughter, Mavis, brought us to The Epicure Wednesday and I filled the freezer with cabbage rolls. I can spare a few for my favorite daughter."

That's what he calls me when he wants a favor. It's also what he calls my sister, Esther, on the rare occasions she phones or visits.

The long, narrow hallway leading to my father's apartment stinks of several generations of boiled beef and cabbage, but when I open his door I detect the pungent aroma of simmering tomatoes and vinegar. He turns down the heat on the stove when he sees me and comes to the door to give me a kiss. Then he follows me into the living room where I plop on the couch.

He plants himself in front of me and shifts from foot to foot, rocking like a dinghy on rough seas. "You notice anything different?"

I play his game, glancing around the small room. The swivel chairs are covered with faded blue sheets. Back issues of *The Forward,* a newspaper he's read in Yiddish since I was a kid, are strewn across the antique pine cocktail table. All as usual. But the bulletin board next to the kitchen, usually plastered with colorful ads for early bird specials, has been covered with neatly arrayed black and white photos. I can't make out the images from where I'm sitting.

"I don't see anything," I say, looking straight at my father. I reach for the newspaper lying on the couch beside me. "Should I?"

He walks to the bulletin board and taps its edge. "You know who this is?"

I get up, grunting, making a big show of the effort it takes and walk to where he's pointing. In seconds, my stomach churns and nausea fills my chest. In the photos, an attractive woman stands on a boat dock, leans against a market stall full of straw baskets and waves from the passenger seat of a 1950s convertible.

She's not my mother.

The woman's skin is light but her features—the fullness of her lips, the curl of her hair—suggest African blood. A snapshot in the middle of the display shows my father sitting with his arm around her on an elegantly-tufted banquette. They're smiling, cheeks pressed against one another. I recognize the restaurant as a once-famous Bahamian nightclub my father brought us to in Nassau one summer on vacation. We had dinner there and I admired the giant jeweled elephant statues that stared at us from shelves around the club. My father—who always used the term *schvartze*, a derogatory Yiddish word for blacks, when he talked about the truck drivers he employed—made a big show of his friendship with the owner, having me shake hands with the darkest man I'd ever seen. I felt intimidated by his deep laugh and his large frame, which seemed to fill the nightclub.

When I turn to my father, I catch a nasty glimmer

in his eyes and a hint of wiseass in the curl of his lip. I wonder if he put the pictures out to brag of his prowess or get my goat. It's a game he plays, daring me to react. I look at the photos and ball my fists, pumping them open and closed. This time he's gone too far. I walk to the bathroom and slam the door. When I'm through splashing water to relieve the heat flushing my cheeks, I look in the mirror.

And there she is. My mother. It's uncanny how much I look like she did at the same age.

For a long time all I felt for Bernice, as I called my mother during my teen years, was contempt. I'm not proud of it but when you're young the world is black and white and you're unwilling or unable to perceive the subtle grays and off-whites that make life bearable. I hated the fact that she took my father back each time he cheated with a new woman. I never considered the fact that my mother was married at twenty-one and a mother of two by twenty-four. And a woman who's spent her life keeping house, raising children and playing tennis at a country club is ill prepared to face the working world. My mother and her friends spoke in the hushed tones they'd use to talk about cancer when they discussed Bunny, a friend who went to work after her husband died.

My mother and father fought late most nights, sending me scurrying for the comfort of my sister's bed when I was little. When we were in our early teens, Mom would call us into her room, sit us down, and solemnly announce she was leaving my father. Esther would get upset, which bugged me no end me because we'd been through this so many times and our mom always stayed. I'd shrug, say go ahead, makes sense to me. Then my mother would glare at me, waiting, and I'd squirm under the pressure of her desperate need for sympathy.

"Rebecca, you okay?" My father bangs on the bathroom door. "I'm heating the stuffed cabbage now."

I splash more water on my face before coming out. He's in the kitchen, adjusting the heat under the open pan. "I want to tell you a little story before we eat," I say. "You want to sit down?"

When he hesitates, I take his arm and gently propel him toward a kitchen chair. He looks confused but sits and I join him.

"You remember the Boopsies?" I ask, referring to what my mother and her girlfriends called their circle of friends. It consisted of four couples from the neighborhood who dined at each others' homes on Saturday nights.

He nods.

"There was this one night, I think I was nine, when mom took Esther and me to meet them at Burger King. *You*," I take a few seconds to emphasize the word, "were in Nassau. On business, I suppose."

He raises an eyebrow but I continue.

"I figured it was just another night without Dad. That was okay with me because we got to eat at Burger King when you were out of town. Mom seemed nervous all day, and yelled at me to do my homework. Usually she wouldn't take us out if we didn't have our homework done, so I was surprised when she told me and Esther to get in the car."

I stop a second to collect my thoughts.

"It must have been October because Esther wore her new yellow sweater with the sunflower buttons. The one you bought her when she turned twelve. When we got to Burger King, Aunt Lacey and Aunt Bunny were already at a table, eating. Mom got Esther and me hamburgers and made us sit at a separate table with the kids. She and her friends sat across the room."

My father smiles, probably remembering how I resented being relegated to the children's table.

"So I was sitting there, fighting with Robbie, who was always telling me how stupid I was, when I looked up. Aunt Lacey had her arm around Mom's shoulders and Mom was crying. I got scared because I thought something happened to you. Maybe your plane crashed. I jumped up and started to head over but Esther grabbed my arm. She told me to stay, that she didn't think Mom wanted us to hear. I hated it when Esther bossed me around. I usually ignored her, but not this time. I was too shocked at seeing Mom cry."

"Do you really need to tell me this?" my father breaks in.

"Fair is fair. I'll listen to your story about that lady," I nod toward the bulletin board, "but I get to talk too."

He shakes his head and sits back, staring through the glass sliding doors toward the concrete slab patio. The only furniture out there is a weather-beaten wicker chair that sat in my parents' bedroom for thirty years. The once-pink cushion is bleached white from years of exposure to the sun and rain.

"I was so upset I couldn't finish my hamburger," I continue. "Mom and Aunt Lacey left the restaurant and went out to the car. I ran to the window to see what they were doing but the parking lot was dark. When I looked up, Aunt Bunny was watching Esther and me and there was pity in her eyes. This was just a few months after Uncle Barry died. And she was looking at *us* with pity. It gave me the creeps.

"By this time, Robbie also noticed our mothers were gone. And you know what he told me? He said he heard Aunt Lacey talking on the phone with Mom that afternoon. She sent him out of the room but he stood outside her door and listened. Robbie told me my dad had a girlfriend and kid in Nassau and that they were black."

My father rises and walks into the kitchen. I stop talking and watch as he gets the flatware out of the drawer, then returns and slams forks and knives onto the placemats. His eyes are red and I fight to suppress a pang of guilt.

"I jumped across the table and punched Robbie so hard his nose bled," I say after my father is seated. "Esther and the other kids had to drag me off him. Aunt Bunny grabbed a bunch of napkins and made Robbie lie down on top of the table and sent Esther out to the car to get Mom and Aunt Lacey. We left when the bleeding stopped.

"Later, in the car, I told Mom why I hit Robbie. She was real quiet. Finally, after I asked four or five times if it was true, she answered. You'll love what she said."

My father remains silent.

"She said you were a good father and that you loved Esther and me and that's what really mattered."

I don't know what to expect from my father. Contrition? Maybe shame? I wouldn't be surprised if he grew angry. Instead, he shakes his head and looks at me with pity.

"Your mother was right."

I arch an eyebrow.

"Sure, I cheated. But it didn't mean a thing and your mother knew it. I loved her and I loved both of you kids. She," he nods toward the bulletin board, "had nothing to do with my girls at home. A man travels a lot, he gets lonely. And I don't have another family, white or black." He laughs. "Why make such a big deal?"

I stare at him, too surprised to speak. I'm jittery with rage. He has no idea what I'm trying to tell him. I've wasted the last half hour explaining something he's incapable of understanding. Can he really be so blind to the pain he caused? Or in denial? Maybe he doesn't care.

"Don't you get it?" I ask. "Don't you know how much it hurt Mom when you cheated? And you were gone all the time, in the Bahamas. You can see how Robbie came up with that idea." I know my questions are falling on deaf ears, but I ask anyway.

"Robbie was an idiot. I had a family to support and I did what it took. If that meant a week or two in the Bahamas every month, so be it." He hesitates, looks toward the bulletin board. "It's not like I had a choice."

"What's that supposed to mean?" I spit out the words.

He glares at me. "It means that you and your mother and sister lived very well, and you have me to thank."

His face takes on a closed look and the angry set to his jaw signals the conversation is over. I'm frustrated and angry but realize there's no point in arguing. If he feels no remorse for cheating on my mother, how can I expect his sympathy over my husband's cheating? Further discussion will lead to an argument. I can't handle that. Right now, I need my father. Friends are one thing but with my kids away at college and Harold out of the picture, I desperately need to be around family.

I walk to the bulletin board and examine the photo in the nightclub. My father looks proud of the attractive woman around whose shoulder his arm is draped. I search for the slightest tinge of guilt or embarrassment. There is none.

"You know what?" I rise from my chair. "My appetite seems to be gone. I'm going to skip dinner. You enjoy the stuffed cabbage."

I grab my purse and step into the kitchen on my way out, leaning over the stove to sniff the sweet and sour scent of cabbage, raisins and meat rising in heady waves from the pot. Unless my nose misleads me, The Epicure uses a splash more vinegar than my mother did. The pungent aroma recalls the smell I often came home to on Friday afternoons. It meant Dad was flying back from a business trip.

When I get home, I open the plastic container of stuffed cabbage I left on the counter to defrost that afternoon. My sons are coming home from college tomorrow for a brief visit. Grandma's stuffed cabbage is one of their favorite meals so there's always a stash in the freezer. But when I open the container to check if it's defrosted, the odor nauseates me. I pour the soupy mixture into the garbage disposal then run the tap and watch the water circle the drain as the metal blades shred the last of the chopped meat and cabbage.

Coloreds Not Served Here

In April 1959, two Jews and two African Americans walked into the Woolworth's on Flagler Street in downtown Miami and took seats at the store's lunch counter. When the waitress spotted them, she disappeared and returned a few minutes later with an assistant manager who announced that Woolworths "does not serve coloreds."

These four Miamians, members of a non-violent civil rights group called CORE, were the first among dozens of blacks and whites to hold lunch counter sit-ins in Miami the same year. Though the road was arduous, their efforts led to small cracks in the wall of bigotry that had made South Florida such a hospitable environment for racism that the Klan's national Grand Wizard viewed Miami as the ideal place to retire in 1945.

In April 1960, a biracial committee that included government officials proposed a plan that called for teams of CORE members to be served lunch at the counters at the W.T. Grant, F.W. Woolworth, and S.H. Kress department stores. Through this agreement, Miami became the first city in Florida to remove racial barriers at lunch counters.

Pearlie Does For Tootsie

The door to my father's apartment is slightly ajar, which is enough to make me nervous in the first place. I rap on it and yell "dad" a few times before pushing it open. There's no response so I step inside and glance around. The old man gets a little cranky when I walk in unannounced. Last time I did that, he started in with this whole *shtick* about how I might've caught him "in flagrantie." I'm fairly sure he means *in flagrante delicto*, naked and in bed with a woman. Having seen the ladies at the Schmuel Bernstein Jewish Home for the Aged, where he lives, I find this laughable. Never mind that he's eighty-six and not in the best of health.

The apartment feels too quiet, too empty. When he called me last Wednesday, I told him I'd come over with dinner on Sunday so I am expected. But the pile of newspapers my dad usually dumps on the stretch of carpet between his couch and cocktail table is missing and the kitchen sink lacks its usual jumble of glasses and bowls. Even the rag he uses to dry dishes is gone from its customary spot over the oven door handle. It's as though my father abandoned the furnished apartment, taking the few objects that mark it as his own. I get a hard feeling at the base of my throat, as though my Adam's apple is swollen. The door to the bedroom's closed and I'm afraid of what I'll find on the other side. That maybe my dad died and no one bothered to tell me before clearing the apartment for the next tenant?

I take a deep breath and open the door.

"Thank God." The words escape in a long breath, louder than I intended. Tootsie rolls over. He opens his eyes and blinks, then reaches across to the nightstand for his glasses.

"Rebecca?"

"Sorry to barge in. I knocked but you didn't answer and the door to the hall was open. Everything okay?"

"What time is it?" he says, glancing at the clock on his side table. "Jeeze, I overslept. I took a nap about three, figured I'd catch an hour or two before you came." He swings his legs over the side of the bed and pushes the covers away. "I told Pearlie to make sure the lock engaged when she left. Guess she forgot."

He sits on the edge of the bed, looking as confused as I feel.

"Pearlie?" I say. "Grandma Yentl's nurse? What was she doing here?"

I haven't heard Pearlie's name in ten years. She's the Jamaican woman who watched over my grandmother for the last two years of her life, caring for her as she sank into dementia.

"Pearlie stops by now and again to see me. We're old friends." He sounds defensive.

I raise an eyebrow which he, naturally, interprets the wrong way.

"It's not what you think."

"That she cleans up?" I laugh.

He gives me a dirty look. "If she wants to pick up here and there, who am I to stop her?"

"So you're having her clean for you now?"

"Nothing like that. It's a social visit. Her apartment's near here and she stops in to see how I'm doing. She still works as a live-in, so we get together when she's off. I try to give her a couple of bucks for helping me clean up but she won't take it."

He stands. "I got to piss and get dressed. You want to make me some coffee. And check that the door's closed."

My father walks into the living room with his pants unzipped and turns his back to me as he tucks in his shirt and belts his trousers. I'm in the kitchen getting out plates for the bagels and lox I picked up for dinner.

"Coffee's brewing if you want some." I say, handing him a glass of orange juice through the pass-through. It's a pleasure reaching into the overhead cabinet and finding a clean glass rather than scouring one that's been sitting in the sink for days. I join him at the kitchen table and set down our bagels, pushing the newspaper out of the way. "So tell me about Pearlie."

"Not much to tell. She's in her early seventies now, still working. She stops by, we talk about my mother, our kids, the usual."

Harold was just starting his medical practice and our boys were small when my grandmother died, so I only had time for occasional visits in her last years. Pearlie was always there and we'd chat briefly. I knew my dad picked up Pearlie and Grandma every Saturday morning and took them to a shopping mall for lunch. The old man claims his long life is a gift from God for being good to his mother.

I think back to the last time I saw Pearlie. It was at my grandmother's funeral, where she seemed even more devastated than my father. I could understand that. She'd been with Grandma Yentl almost non-stop for two years. I was surprised, though, when she didn't return to the house after the funeral.

I tell my dad as much. "You'd think that in her profession, she'd learn to cope with loss. Most of the people she cares for must be pretty old and sick."

I look up from my plate when he doesn't answer. My father averts his eyes. "What's wrong?" I ask.

"What do you mean?"

I'm not sure how to answer. I sense there's something he's not saying. "First, I come over and the house is cleaned up. Then you tell me Pearlie—whom you haven't mentioned in years—pays you regular visits. What else don't I know?"

I wait for an answer, but he stares through the sliding glass doors to what the Schmuel Bernstein, in its promotional material, calls The Phyllis and Marvin Teitelbaum Memorial Garden. It's nothing more than a black-tarred walkway that winds around scruffy groupings of coconut palms and ixora. The gardener planted impatiens that week and the flowers form scraggly pink and white splashes at the base of the palms. Across a small clearing, two middle-aged black women in white uniforms sit on plastic chairs under a wooden trellis behind their wheelchair-bound charges.

"Come on, Dad. Something's going on."

"Such as?"

"Look, if you don't want to tell me, fine." I rise from my seat. "I can call Pearlie myself. I'm sure she's in the phone book."

"Will you take it easy? It's no big deal." My father hesitates. When he speaks, his words come out slowly, as though he's debating each syllable. "This may sound crazy, but Pearlie may blame herself for Grandma's death."

"Why?"

"You know how grandma died?"

"Heart failure?"

"Honest to God, Rebecca, you can be so stupid. Everyone dies of heart failure."

"About Pearlie?" I say, directing him back on topic.

"You remember how the floors in Grandma's apartment were uneven?"

I nod.

"When Grandma needed a wheelchair, we installed a wooden ramp between the bedroom and bathroom so it would be easier to roll her over the drop. Pearlie had just taken Grandma to the bathroom and hadn't bothered to belt her back in the chair, figuring she was going straight to bed. When she rolled Grandma over the ramp, Grandma slumped over and fell out of the wheelchair. She broke her leg. Pearlie called me and I arrived as the paramedics were leaving. I told Pearlie to stay behind and I'd follow the ambulance."

He rises and takes our plates to the sink. When he returns to the table, he folds the newspaper, then arranges the napkins in their holder so they're perfectly aligned.

"What happened to Grandma?"

"Her leg became infected and the infection spread through her body. Her kidneys went and then her lungs and heart and, *mitten dritten*, she was gone. It all happened in less than two days."

"All that from a broken leg?"

He hesitates. "More or less."

"What's that mean?"

"Oy, Rebecca, you ask too many questions."

"I don't have a right to know how my grandmother died?"

"All right." He places his hands on the table and leans in toward me. I'm accosted by the brackish odor of smoked salmon and coffee. "I mentioned your grandmother, of blessed memory, slumped before she fell out of the chair?"

"Yeah."

"She had a sudden, massive stroke. She was probably brain dead before she hit the floor." He rises and walks to the sliding glass doors that lead to his tiny cement patio, turning his back to me.

"Does Pearlie know that?"

He lifts his shoulders, drops them. "I don't remember."

"How can you not remember?"

"It's been a long time. I think I told her."

I stare at my father. Did he really forget? It's possible. My grandmother's been gone for almost ten years. But if Pearlie doesn't know, she may feel guilty about the death. Is that why my father hasn't mentioned his friendship with Pearlie? He's afraid I'll tell her the truth and Pearlie will abandon him.

I'm about to question my father when I notice how fragile he looks. Standing in profile against the sliding glass doors, his back forms a curve, a slight ellipsis. I visit my father almost every week so I don't notice him aging. It's such a gradual process. But tonight it's as if this elderly stranger has superimposed himself on the vigorous middle-aged man I imagine my father to be.

"You should tell her," I say, torn between tenderness and contempt.

"What's the big deal? Dead is dead. Doesn't matter how it happened."

"Of course it does. If you don't tell Pearlie, I will." In case he doesn't get it, "Why should she live with that guilt?"

I rise and grab my purse off the kitchen counter before leaving. I usually wash his dishes. Today I don't. After all, he has Pearlie.

The next Sunday evening, when I pull to the entrance of the Schmuel Bernstein, Pearlie is waiting with Tootsie. I'm stunned. My father's taken me up on my threat.

Pearlie is thin and angular and the knotted muscles of her forearms look hard and shiny beneath her deep brown skin. Tootsie wears his usual baggy khakis and a polo shirt, but Pearlie is dressed for a night on the town. Her white cotton shirtwaist is a style I haven't seen in decades and a red patent leather belt fits neatly around her waist. A red hat, perched on what is obviously a wig, emphasizes the broad bone structure of her face. It's remarkable how little she's changed.

The two ease themselves out of the plastic lawn chairs on the front porch and Pearlie slides her arm through Tootsie's in a gesture that could be companionship or support. I get out of the car and go around to give each a kiss. Pearlie envelops me in a big hug.

"Rebecca," she sings out, pronouncing each syllable with the same emphasis as my father. She puts a hand on each of my shoulders and smiles. "Look at you." I wait for a compliment. It doesn't come. "When your father said you'd invited me to join you for dinner, I was so delighted."

"I'm glad you could make it." I turn to my dad, who is grinning from ear to ear. "Where should we go?"

"I thought that we'd drive down to The Circus Diner," he says, then adds, "if that's okay with you. It's one of the places we took Grandma and Pearlie hasn't been there in years."

It's a half hour drive, but I agree. We chat on the way over about her work. She tells me she's between jobs, but lived with an elderly woman until she died two weeks earlier.

The Circus Diner is one of my father's favorite restaurants, the place we went for birthdays when I was growing up. We could count on the waiters to circle the table and sing happy birthday, usually in an assortment of foreign accents. It hasn't changed. From the outside, the shiny chrome and corrugated aluminum structure looks like something from the set of a 1950s' movie, with all the curves and sharp angles of a fifty-three Chevy. The interior is small and unassuming and the white linen tablecloths appear incongruous in so modest a space. But the food is great and really fresh.

My father and I sit in a booth together, with Pearlie opposite. I'm edgy, wondering how Pearlie will react if

I tell her the truth. When she opens her menu, I look at my father with my eyebrows raised. He meets my gaze and flashes a grin. I can't believe it. He's calling my bluff.

He reaches across the table and taps Pearlie's menu. "You should try the swordfish," he says, "grilled with lime."

During dinner, Pearlie asks about my two sons, whom she's kept up with through my father. I tell her they're doing well in college and she says her grandson graduated from the University of Florida last spring.

Once the waiter removes our plates, I clean my eyeglasses and struggle with how to tell Pearlie about my grandmother's death. I don't know whether to apologize or insist Tootsie do so himself. I'm livid at my father for forcing me to reveal what he's done and afraid Pearlie will become upset and insist we take her home.

I cough and clear my throat before speaking. "I think you should know why Dad and I invited you out. Besides, of course, wanting to see you."

She looks up, smiles.

"You know how grandma died after falling out of her wheelchair?"

"Of course."

"I don't think my dad ever told you that Grandma had a stroke before she fell. That's *why* she fell out of her wheelchair. It had nothing to do with you." I'm trying to find words to absolve her of guilt. "She was probably brain dead when she hit the floor and would've died anyway."

I sit back and wait for the worst. She looks at my father, her lips pressed together, then back at me. Her eyebrows gather across her forehead to form a single gray brow and I feel like a student sent to the principal's office, awaiting her verdict. Will she storm out of the restaurant? Tell off my father? My stomach cramps in anticipation. I'm stunned when she leans back in her chair and laughs. "Har, har, har." It's a loud, hearty from-the-gut sound. The waiters look over from the soccer game they're watching behind the bar and smile, as does my father. I'm stumped. What's so damned funny?

"Honey, don't be silly. I don't blame myself," Pearlie says. "I've been taking care of old folks so long I can just about predict when they're going to pass. Your grandma was an old lady, bless her heart, and it was her time to go. Didn't much matter how. I do my best. After that it's the Lord's work."

I look at her, then at Tootsie. "So why . . ." I don't know how to finish the question. I feel like a fool.

"She doesn't think her father has any friends," Tootsie says. Then he turns to me. "I do have *some* good qualities, despite what *you* think. Which always seems to be the worst. Well, doll, you're way off base this time." He speaks quickly and insistently and I suspect he's as surprised as I am by her reaction. "Pearlie's an old friend and we enjoy each other's company."

I've got to hand it to the old man. He knows how to pull a fast recovery.

A wave of heat creeps up my neck. I can't meet my father's gaze or Pearlie's.

"Is that what this is all about?" Pearlie reaches across the table and takes my hand. Her skin is rough and her broad hand envelops mine. "You think I visit your daddy out of guilt? You young people don't understand a lot of things." I grin. No one's called me a young person in quite a while. "Now, you know your father and I got to be good friends taking your grandma out. He's a good man and we had a good time. You don't just stop being friends, like it's a job that ends when your patient dies. What kind of person would I be if I did that?"

"But why clean his house?" I play my only card.

"You've seen what a pig sty that is." Then to my father, "No offense meant." He grins as though proud of his slovenliness. "I help my old friends. I clean. You cook for your daddy and take him out. Same thing. You do what you can for the people you love."

When dessert comes, Tootsie launches into a ten-minute tirade on the lousy weather we're having and how the *schmuck* next door won't lower the volume of his television set. I'm sick of hearing it, but she listens patiently.

Tootsie spills fudge on his shirt and leaves for the bathroom to wash it off just as the waiter drops our check on the table. "Don't touch that," he says. "I'll be right back to pay." I hand the waiter my credit card.

Pearlie leans across the table and pats my hand. "Honey, don't you worry about your daddy. He's a fine man and wouldn't take advantage of a flea. He was good to his mother and that says a lot. Just like you're good to him."

As Tootsie nears the table, she winks. Her hair's a bit crooked and she puts her hands on top of her hat to adjust the red fedora. The entire hat and wig apparatus shift to the left. "You treat your father fine and the Lord will provide."

My father arrives at the same time the waiter returns with my credit card. When he sees me signing the check, he returns his wallet to his back pocket. "Okay, Miss Smartypants," he says as Pearlie and I rise. "You ready to head back with your popular father?"

Driving them home, I realize how off base I've been. Maybe my father is taking advantage of Pearlie. Maybe not. It's none of my business. What matters is that the two are friends and take care of each other. And that transcends any judgments I thought I had the right to make.

A Slap in the Face to Miami Blacks

In 1990, shortly after his historic release from prison by South Africa's white minority government, Nelson Mandela came to Miami to address a conference. Instead of presenting him with a key to the city, an honor traditionally bestowed on visiting dignitaries, Miami's City Commission rescinded its proclamation welcoming the South African hero. Mandela had committed what leaders of Miami's Cuban community considered the heinous sin of supporting Fidel Castro. Jews in South Florida also were alarmed at Mandela's support of Yasser Arafat.

Castro and Arafat were among the few leaders to support Mandela's anti-apartheid movement.

Miami African Americans, who made up about one fifth of the city's residents, considered the Mandela snub a slap in the face. The commission's action was particularly galling as it followed decades of economic, social and political insults and uneasy relations between Miami's African American and Cuban communities. In response, several black Miami leaders called for an economic boycott against the tourism industry. African American groups, in particular, were urged to take their conventions and vacations elsewhere. In its first year, the boycott cost Miami an estimated $27 million in convention business.

The boycott ended in 1992 with Miami political and business leaders agreeing to a 20-point plan that included an investigation into a 1990 incident of police brutality against Haitian protesters, higher-level tourism jobs for African Americans and creation of a black-owned convention hotel in Miami Beach. That year, then-Miami Dade Mayor Alex Pinelas also apologized to the NAACP for his predecessors' actions.

Guns and Latkes: A Chanukah Tale

The earthy orange scent of turmeric greets me as I step off the elevator to my father's floor at the Schmuel Bernstein. I haven't seen Tootsie in a month and wonder if a new resident, an Arabic Jew, has moved in and is toiling over exotic stews in her kitchen. I picture a tiny woman with stark black hair and wrinkled hands pinching dough and sautéing eggplant for mouth-watering bourekas. I'm on the lookout for exotic food stories and make a mental note to stop by during my next visit. The cilia in my nose quiver as I pass the apartment.

"Let yourself in," the old man yells when I knock on his door, "and leave my gifts on the hall table.

I can tell he's been hard at work because the rich aroma of shredded potatoes crisping in peanut oil greets me in his hallway and the white apron stretched across his belly is splotched with grease. Truth be told, Tootsie's latkes are a lot tastier than the frozen hockey pucks my mother bought at the grocery when we were kids. Latkes are one of the few recipes my father got from his own mother and I appreciate the effort he puts into making them. I kiss his cheek and reach for one of the crispy potato pancakes he's set out to drain on a paper towel next to the frying pan. He's in the middle of a batch and the potatoes look like miniature golden-brown bird nests bubbling in oil.

"Take a look at your Chanukah present," he says, motioning toward the kitchen table with a spatula.

A small box, wrapped in blue and white striped paper with dancing dreidels, sits dead center on the table surrounded by placemats and flatware. I pick it up and feel its heft in the palm of my hand. It's solid and heavy for such a small package. When I tilt the box, nothing shifts.

Tootsie comes around the kitchen counter and stands across the table from me. He hugs his chest, hands tucked into his armpits, and rocks back and forth in an apparent agony of anticipation. "You going to open it?"

"What's the big hurry?"

"Just open the damned thing."

I tear the colorful paper away to find a brown cardboard box sealed with masking tape. Once that's off, I have to disentangle the gift from crumpled sheets of aged, yellowing newspaper. I expect to find a paper weight for my collection.

Instead, I find a gun.

I'm so surprised I nearly drop the weapon on the table. I've never held a gun before and the cold, hard steel feels foreign and dangerous in my hand. It's an ugly little snub-nosed revolver, shiny stainless steel at the barrel with a dark walnut grip.

"What is this?" I ask, placing the weapon on the table. "Is it loaded?"

My dad picks up the gun, spins the cylinder, and delivers the verdict: "Empty." He sets it back on the table and looks at me out of the corner of his eyes. A smile edges his lips. Something's up.

"All right," I say. "You want to tell me what this is about? You know I hate guns."

"You don't recognize it?" He snorts. "It's the gun your Uncle Moe gave me after we opened our store near Overtown. I showed it to your mother and she wasn't pleased. But it was a rough neighborhood. Lots of whores and pimps hanging out on the corners. Moe and I both kept guns in our office."

"Why'd you move into such a lousy area?"

"That's where all the restaurant supply showrooms were. People would fly into Miami from the islands and head straight to Miami Avenue for their restaurant supplies."

"Did you ever use it?" I motion toward the gun with my chin.

He looks at it, then back at me. His smile is gone. "I almost blew off a *schvartze's* head with this gun."

I cringe at the term. He misinterprets my reaction as disbelief.

"You heard me right. Your mother knew about it. And your sister. You were probably gone by then. Everyone had a gun. I got it just before the riots in nineteen eighty."

I work out the numbers. I'd been married three years by then and lived in Cincinnati.

"Mom never told me a thing," I say. "Was that when those Hispanic cops got off after killing a black guy?"

"You got it. Even I was shocked by the verdict. Talk about timing. The Marielitos were pouring in from Cuba and stealing jobs from the blacks. You remember

Mary, colored lady used to manage the books?"
I nod.

"She threatened to leave if I hired a Cuban. Can you believe that? Works for me ten years and says she'll work with whites or blacks, but any Cubans, she's out of there. Back then, you had a choice. Now you got to speak Spanish to get a table at a restaurant."
He isn't entirely wrong.

"We were only a few blocks away from where the police killed the guy. Fellow named McCormack, McDuffie, something like that." He shakes his head. "It was a rough area. No cop wanted to work those streets. Your Uncle Moe and I bought a block of buildings in the neighborhood and turned the largest one into our showroom. Cops would stop by, tell us we were nuts to be in the area."

"They knew you had a gun?"

"No reason to mention it. I kept it in a drawer, locked. I didn't want trouble from the neighborhood but, if it came, we were prepared."

I recognize the acrid odor of burning oil at the same moment he jumps up and follow him into the kitchen, where he pulls the smoking pan off the burner. He removes the blackened latkes, pours the hot oil into a coffee can and starts over with fresh peanut oil.

"We got along with the neighbors," he says, dropping clumps of grated potato mixture into the oil. "But Miami was a mess. Cubans sleeping under bridges and in stadiums. You couldn't step outside downtown without tripping over a refugee."

He pushes the latkes around in the pan, where they float in sizzling oil. When they're golden brown, he loads them onto a plate and hands it to me. I take it to the table and he follows with the bowls of apple sauce and sour cream he takes out of the refrigerator. The gun awaits us in the middle of the table, an ugly, menacing centerpiece. We sit.

He spoons a dollop of sour cream on a latke before continuing. "So one night around midnight, I got a call. The alarm at the store went off and the cops contacted Moe, who called me. I jumped in the car and headed up Dixie. I couldn't believe what I saw. You know how Dixie Highway rises as it turns into I-95?"

"Near Bay Heights?"

He nods. "I went up that hill, drove a mile and saw a wall of grey smoke hovering over downtown Miami, mostly to the west. As I neared the office, I realized the smoke was billowing up from Overtown. I later learned rioters set a tire factory on fire. Didn't bother to loot it first. Just destroyed it for the hell of it. I got off the expressway near my office and ran into a half dozen men beneath an underpass. Several held baseball bats so I got out of there fast, never mind the lights. I hadn't listened to the news so didn't know the cops who'd killed McDuffie got off that day. The blacks went nuts. I heard later that a couple of thugs dragged a white kid out of his car and beat him to death."

"Weren't you scared?" I say, shuddering at the image of my dad alone in a car surrounded by an angry mob.

"You better believe it. A cop was waiting in front of our store when I got there. Another was inside. I don't know if my brother paid them off to guard us. They should've been in Overtown, controlling the riot. When I got inside, I found Moe standing over this black kid, maybe twenty, and pointing a gun at his head. He told me the boy tried to break in through our roof but fell through the skylight. The kid lay on the floor surrounded by glass shards, with his arm twisted at a weird angle. He was a skinny kid and looked like a child, sobbing in fright or pain—probably both."

Tootsie curls his lip. "You know what my brother, that son-of-a-bitch, did?"

I shake my head.

"He handed me the gun and said, 'I got a rap sheet, you don't.' I stood there like a *shmuck* until it hit me. Moe wanted *me* to shoot the kid.

"Uncle Moe actually asked you . . ." I'm horrified. My uncle was a coarse man who used foul language, but I couldn't imagine him killing a defenseless human being.

"I was as shocked as you are. I looked at one of the cops, a fat-faced Mick not much older than the kid on the floor. I figured he'd tell Moe to lay off. Instead, he tells me I have a right to protect my property. I couldn't believe it. Sure, the kid broke into the business I spent my life building. But to murder him?"

"Did you let him go?"

My father looks at me, narrowing his eyes. "Of course I did. What the hell kind of person you think I am. I was mad all right. But not at the kid. At Moe. He was five years older than me and, like an idiot, I always listened to him. But this was sick. I grabbed the gun out of his hand, walked into my office, and locked it in my drawer. Then I came back and told the cops to get the kid out of there before I killed *them*."

"I'm surprised they didn't arrest you."

The old man grunts. "Fat chance. I called an ambulance and they brought the boy out on a stretcher.

After the cops left, I gave Moe a piece of my mind. He claimed he used the gun to frighten the intruder and never intended to fire it. Acted like it was a big joke. The idiot. We locked up and went home."

"You think Uncle Moe would've killed the kid?"

"You didn't know your uncle if you need to ask."

He's got a point. My uncle was good to me and, as far as I knew, an affectionate husband and father. But I was a child when he died and most of my memories of him are at holiday dinners and birthday parties.

"Why'd you give this to me?" I ask, picking up the gun and setting it back in the box. "What am I supposed to do with it?"

"Nothing." He laughs. "Kill your ex. I don't know what I was thinking. I found it last night while cleaning out the closet in my bedroom. I wanted to see how you'd react."

That's quite an admission. Pissing me off then watching me sputter is one of his favorite pastimes.

"I should've dumped it years ago. Your Uncle Moe's gone. The cops we met that night are probably six feet under. I guess you could call it a memento of Miami history. A lesson in business one-o-one."

"What do you mean?"

He rises from the table and takes our plates to the sink.

"You think you're doing some good, hiring people, helping the community. But after a while you realize no one gives a damn. We knew we were taking a chance, buying property near Overtown. The cops warned us to be careful. I figured we'd be fine. Treat our neighbors fairly. Be treated fairly in return. It didn't happen that way. Most people in the neighborhood were fine. But a couple of animals ruined it for everyone. A few days before the riot we hid a prostitute in the store when her pimp came looking for her with a baseball bat. She was on the street the next morning. Then this break in." He shrugs.

I finish clearing the table, then drop the gun in my purse.

"You going to keep that thing?" my father asks.

"You gave it to me."

"Don't be ridiculous. I'll get rid of it."

He reaches for my purse, but I pull it away.

I pat the side of my bag, where the gun is lodged, and walk to the door. "It's mine now."

My purse feels heavy when I sling it onto my ancient Mercedes' passenger seat. I head south on Biscayne Boulevard, over the Miami River and past the towering marble and glass behemoths that line Brickell Avenue. After a few miles, the skyscrapers give way to elegantly landscaped estates and I pull off the road into a park that faces onto the bay. It's nearly dark and I don't spot another soul as I cross a grassy field to the water's edge.

More than twenty years have passed since the McDuffie trial and the break-in at my dad's store. We've gotten past the riots, the Mariel boatlifts and the cocaine cowboys who put Miami on the map with their cigarette boats and drug running. We're much more civilized now. Black and white relations aren't perfect but we're well beyond the days of separate bathrooms and water fountains, of riots in the streets.

At least that's what I'd like to believe.

Across the bay, Key Biscayne is a faint grid of lights on the horizon. The gentle splash of waves against the rocky shore and the distant hum of a skiff motoring to safe harbor are the only sounds. I pull the gun out of my purse and reach back to build leverage in my right arm. Then I release the solid metal projectile into the air. The stainless steel glints in the moonlight as it arcs up then drops toward Biscayne Bay. It makes a faint splash as it hits the water.

Cops Like a Pack of Wild Dogs

The Miami riots of 1980 broke out on a steamy Saturday afternoon in May when police and African American youths exchanged gunfire in the predominantly black neighborhood of Liberty City. A few hours earlier, a Tampa jury had acquitted four white Miami policemen accused of beating and killing a black Miami insurance salesman, Arthur McDuffie. The jury was all white.

No one was surprised by the community's outrage. A medical examiner described the trauma to the 33-year-old man's skull as equivalent to that of a four-story fall. He testified that McDuffie's head was beaten so severely against the pavement that it created a ten-inch star-like pattern across the back of his skull.

The officers charged with the crime claimed McDuffie's injuries occurred when he was thrown from his motorcycle during a police chase. People on the scene said the officers refused to accept McDuffie's surrender and rammed his motorcycle with a police cruiser to create the appearance of an accident. Witnesses compared the officers beating McDuffie to "a pack of wild dogs attacking a piece of meat."

When the riots were over, 18 were dead and $100 million in property damage had been done, primarily to businesses in African American neighborhoods. Many of the ruined properties belonged to Jewish businessmen who owned area grocery stores, pawn shops, import/export companies and appliance emporiums.

McDuffie's beating couldn't have come at a worse time. Miami was struggling with a massive influx of Cuban refugees—125,000 immigrants, 26,000 of them with prison records—who were taking the jobs and social benefits traditionally taken by African Americans. Decades earlier, the once culturally-rich center of Miami's black community had been bisected by Interstate 95. On May 17, 1980, the day the Tampa jury found the McDuffie defendants not guilty, thousands of Cuban refugees were being housed in tents beneath this expressway.

The McDuffie family eventually received a $1.1 million settlement from the Dade County Commission. After a threatened walkout by the Fraternal Order of Police, the city rehired the accused policemen, who were later tried and found not guilty of federal civil rights violations.

The Druid in Purple Knee Boots

It's a blustery Sunday morning and I've had a hard time convincing my father to leave the safe, dry confines of his apartment. I've been working on a series about Florida wineries all weekend and am dying for the eggs and lox at Wasserstein's Deli Nosh. He finally agrees to join me for breakfast but spends the whole meal complaining. His sciatica's acting up. The bastard next door plays his television too loud. The janitor forgot to mop the front hall. I'm as eager to get him home as I was to take him out.

The rain passed earlier in the morning but the winds are still high. I take my time making the return trip across the small bridges that link the man-made islands connecting Miami Beach to downtown Miami. To either side of us, waves kick up white scrims of foam and toss them about Biscayne Bay, which looks glum and forbidding beneath the overcast sky. We pass island after island of extravagant homes behind which fishing boats and yachts bob in the current. Finally, the land narrows and the homes fall behind. One last glimpse of skyline and we're back in the gritty streets of Miami. Modern metallic skyscrapers loom above us as we drive down Fifteenth Street, but the filthy puddles along the curb and faceless men asleep in doorways entrances expose the grimy underside of the city.

I'm braking for a red light when my father grabs my arm and yells, "pull over." I yank the wheel to the right as a character in a full length green coat and purple knee boots walks by the passenger-side door. About half of Miami's homeless look like nomads who've wandered out of medieval computer games with names like "Moonstone" or "Lords of the Realm." This character, with his greasy shoulder-length hair and monk-like cape, could be a warlock or an orc. He mutters and waves a rolled newspaper in the air as if invoking a magical incantation.

"I can't believe that son of a bitch didn't recognize me," my father says. He lowers his window and sticks his head out. I hold my breath, afraid he'll call the scruffy character to the car. The old man reaches for the door handle, but thinks better of it and leans back in his seat. "Dumb n...," he whispers, then lets out a snort that turns into a spasm of coughing. I glare at my father. He knows I hate that kind of language but glances at me and laughs. "Don't look so shocked. He nearly cost my life," he says and motions with his thumb in the direction the druid took.

"What are you talking about?" It's hard to envision the scrawny scarecrow of a druid endangering anyone's life. "Who is he?"

"I should remember his name." My father rolls the window back up. "It was a fag name. Percy, I think. But it's been at least eight years. The bastard, a curse on his head, should rot in hell. It's his fault we were robbed."

"At the house?"

"God, where you been? No, at my *store*." He nods

in the direction of the business he owned for fifty years in downtown Miami. It's only a few blocks from where I'm pulled over. "I never told you?"

I shake my head. It must have happened while I was in college. Most family news came through my mother and she wouldn't have wanted to worry me.

"You must have forgot. I sure didn't. I'm sitting in my office, on the phone, when these goons come in with guns. Stockings over their faces, the whole deal. Two of them go into the showroom and make the girls lie on the floor while they lock the front door. I don't know what's happening until this gorilla comes barreling into my office and points a gun at my head."

I open my mouth but a horn blasts behind us. My father and I look back. I'm so shocked by his story that I don't realize I've blocked traffic. I turn right on to Biscayne Boulevard and look for the druid. The streets are empty.

"I swear to God, Rebecca, I saw my life pass before my eyes. The bastards were in the store ten, maybe fifteen minutes, but it felt like years. They knew where the safe was and held a gun to my head while I emptied it. It was a Friday, pay day." He puts a hand to his chest, takes a deep breath. "I was sure I'd have a heart attack right there. The bastards would've been charged with murder. And the cops would've *had* to do something." He motions with his head out the window. "The asshole who just passed us worked for me then. He let the bastards in."

"He admitted it?"

"Are you kidding?"

"Was he arrested?"

"Arrested?" He cocks an eyebrow. "I couldn't

prove it. Percy was working in the back of the store, doing inventory. He said he forgot to lock the rear doors and the robbers rushed him. My ass. He probably set the whole thing up. Told the bastards where I kept the pay roll."

"So you fired him?"

"Where you been the last century? You can't fire a *black* person. The government's all over you for discrimination. Unless you can prove he's a felon, you're stuck paying unemployment or workmen's comp."

"I can't believe you kept him around."

"I didn't want to but I had no proof he did it, and the cops weren't knocking themselves out over a robbery."

"How'd you get rid of him?"

"That's what pisses me off. The son of a bitch had incredible nerve."

It occurs to me that anyone who wanders Miami streets in that purple druid getup has incredible something.

"What happened?"

"He sued me."

"For what?"

My father gets this crafty look. "For calling him a dumb n . . ."

Again with the N word!

"You said that to his face?"

"Not exactly."

My father removes his glasses, cleans them with the bottom of his tee shirt, then returns them to his nose. "I forgot to put my hand over the mouthpiece on my cell phone."

I throw him a quick glance.

"You heard me. I was at the post office and called the store on my cell. The son of a bitch answered. I wanted an address and told him where to look for it. Naturally, the lazy bastard couldn't be bothered so he came back on the phone and said he couldn't find it. ' Dumb n . . .' came out before I could cover the mouthpiece."

I laugh. The idea of his being sued for what he considered normal behavior is pretty ironic. I've always been perplexed by my father's attitude toward black people. If they're friends or customers, they're Negro or black. If they're street people or employees, they're *schvartzes*. I'd never heard him use the N word and it sounds obscene.

"It's not funny," my father breaks in. "The son of a bitch took me for $3,000. Called in the EEOC or whoever, claimed I was harassing him. I almost went to court. The lawyer told me to settle up. The only good thing was it got the bastard out of my life. That's what he wanted, you know. Money. I didn't have to fire him, which I probably couldn't have done anyway. Once he got enough, he was gone. The Afro-American," he glares at me, emphasizing the politically-correct term, "probably spent it on drugs."

I hate that side of my father—the bigot. It's a part of him that slips into my subconscious when I least expect it. I'd never use those slurs, but they are indelibly etched in my memory. I've heard them my whole life. I try to understand where he's coming from. The son of immigrant Jews, he spent years as an outsider—a greenhorn forced to prove himself to the Irish, the Italians and the African Americans in a tough neighborhood on New York's Lower East Side. Enough of that, you can't get past the idea of them versus us. And after eighty years, you don't care whose feelings or political sensibilities you offend.

I wonder if that's what makes me laugh. The fact that he's *not* embarrassed at the use of the "N" word. Or that he got in trouble for using it.

I'm about to tell my father as much when I spot the druid. He's at a curb a half block up and waves the rolled-up newspaper in front of him as though conducting an orchestra. I slow down, curious about what my father will do. "You want me to hit him?" I joke. Then I speed up and pass the man.

"He's not worth it," my father says as he cranes his neck around to peer through the rear window. "Dumb n . . . got what he had coming."

Miami Blacks Swim

World War II, the same force that revived Miami's flagging economy at the end of the Great Depression with its influx of soldiers, brought limited gains to Miami's African American community. Afraid they'd be forced to allow black soldiers to use whites-only public beaches, the Dade County Commission in 1944 gave the Navy temporary use of the beach at Virginia Key to train black sailors.

African Americans who lived in South Florida responded by demanding a permanent blacks-only beach. A group led by Father Theodore R. Gibson, pastor of Christ Episcopal Church and later a county commissioner, tested the black community's right to use public beaches by swimming at whites-only Baker's Haulover Beach in May 1945.

To prevent further attempts at beach integration, the commission designated Virginia Key a beach for blacks. Within two weeks of this designation, nearly four thousand African American people had visited.

A Rock or a Grasshopper

"Your Aunt Clare doesn't know if she's a rock or a grasshopper," my father says as he reaches for the door handle. I grab his arm and motion him to stay put. We're parked in front of the S&S Diner in downtown Miami and I refuse to get out before the homeless character seated on the sidewalk in front of the restaurant calms down. I don't mind sharing a good laugh, but the black woman blocking the diner is having a riotous conversation with thin air. She's slapping her thighs and rocking back and forth in glee, apparently getting a huge kick out of her imaginary friend. It's hard enough getting through to my dad, whose hearing seems to have worsened in the two weeks since I've seen him. I'm not in the mood to struggle through a conversation with a homeless schizophrenic.

The temperature is in the sixties but I keep the windows up and the air conditioner running. The woman notices us and waves at my father. He returns the wave and adds a thumbs up. I'm taken aback, then realize that he probably knows the woman from when he had his business in the neighborhood. It's hard to believe anyone could survive on the streets for the five years since he retired. It's a gritty neighborhood of abandoned buildings and I figure I'm amassing karma just driving my father down its dusty, potholed streets. Tootsie had breakfast at this diner almost daily for fifty years, stopping on his way to hand out dry socks and crackers to the homeless people he got to know along Northeast Second Avenue.

I've just returned from reporting on a wine festival and visiting an elderly aunt in California and haven't seen the old man in two weeks. So when I show up at his apartment this morning and he announces a hankering for the S&S's food, I can't say no.

"Aunt Clare swears your mother came over on the Lusitania," I say, continuing the conversation we started when I picked him up. "She says it was in 1915, the year before Aunt Irene was born."

"I never heard that," he says, and I see him doing the math in his head. Aunt Irene would've been eighty-five this year.

"That was the same year a German U-boat sunk the Lusitania. So if Aunt Clare's right, Grandma was on the boat's last successful crossing."

"The old broad's crazy. I would've known about that."

"Maybe she didn't tell you."

He thinks a moment, then twists his lips. "Maybe not."

Although we never discussed it, we both know my Grandma Yentl never lost the fearful mentality of the *schtetl* in which she was born. She spoke only Yiddish and relied on her husband to interpret the world for her—to take her shopping, banking, and to the doctor. She discouraged any discussion of the past, a desire we honored because of the tears that welled up at any mention of Russia, where she was born. When my parents told her they were visiting Russia, Grandma became hysterical. The only words I understood through her torrent of emotion were "Cossack" and "murderer."

The homeless lady collects the plastic bags that lie at her feet and rises. She talks to herself as she crams them into her grocery cart, but the laughter and smiles are gone. She takes a few minutes to rearrange her possessions, then heads north, rolling the overstuffed metal cart down the wind-swept, Sunday-deserted street.

On weekday mornings, the horseshoe-shaped counter at S&S is mobbed. Lawyers and businessmen with ties flung over their shoulders hunch over fried eggs and omelets. Rumors have it that in the 1950s, gangsters would sit on one side of the counter, cops on the other, and leave each other alone. I'm surprised to spot an early painting by a popular Miami artist leaning against a window—then remember hearing he often paid for meals with his art. Today, we're the only customers in the place and Tootsie spends a minute or two reminiscing with Irma, a waitress almost as old as he is, before we order pancakes.

"Anyway," I say when she walks to the end of the counter and slaps our order on the pass-through window, "Aunt Clare says that your mother almost didn't make it off the boat, that when your father came to pick her up, they wouldn't let her go because she wasn't married."

"That's not true."

"This is according to her sister. She'd know. She said girls from Europe who didn't have family to claim them sometimes ended up as prostitutes. The government was looking out for them."

I wait for him to object. He doesn't.

"You know that organization that you're always sending money to? The Hebrew International Aid Society? Grandpa Leo had to go to them for help. They arranged for the captain of the Lusitania to marry Grandma and Grandpa. Isn't that wild. Good thing he thought of going to HIAS. She could have been shipped back on the final voyage. The one that was torpedoed."

The waitress tops off our coffees and I wait until she's gone to continue. "Can you imagine? You wouldn't have been born."

When I look up from stirring the cream into my coffee, I'm taken aback by his pained expression. It never occurred to me that the story would cause him the distress I can read in the blackness of his eyes and the set of his jaw.

"Dad, I'm sorry. I thought it was an interesting story. I had no idea . . ."

"You never do, do you Rebecca. Jesus, sometimes I wonder if your mother raised a moron. Aunt Clare, a curse on her head, is a *yenta*. Probably saw a television show about the Lusitania and, in her demented way, made it your grandmother's story."

There's no use arguing so I go back to my pancakes. I've been on a bit of a pancake run lately, trying out different recipes, and notice these include buttermilk and baking soda. I start to mention this when my father pushes his plate away and speaks.

"I didn't want to call while you were in California but something happened while you were gone." His tone blends sarcasm and accusation. I'm taken aback, then realize he was silent during our drive to S&S. I've been so busy jabbering about my trip that I haven't asked about him.

"What? Are you okay?"

"I'm fine, nothing to worry about. A little stroke."

"Oh, Dad." I reach for his hand, but he withdraws it to his lap.

"Don't get all worked up. It was nothing major. I pressed the call button in my apartment when I felt weak and, from what the paramedics told me, I was disoriented a couple minutes. They took me to the emergency room, ran some tests. I was home the next day."

"Did you follow up with Dr. Rosenberg?"

"I went in last Monday. He says I'm okay and wants to increase my Lipitor. I'm going back in two weeks."

I feel terrible. His health, knock wood, has been good so far. One of the tough things about growing close to an aging parent, especially if your other parent is gone, is the fear and dread of losing him. You know you'll regret not spending time together, that you'll comfort yourself with the words, "We were close in those last years." But, at the end of the day, you're taking a risk. There's a push and pull to the relationship, an acceptance and rejection of the inevitability of death that propels it forward. Your sister or brother will lose a parent when he dies. You'll lose a friend.

I gaze at my father out the corner of my eye. His plate is empty. He dips the fingers of both hands in his glass of water, then wipes them on his napkin before taking a drink. I look around to see if the waitress noticed. She's muttering into her cell phone at the end of the counter, her back toward us.

"So what happens now," I ask. "Do you have to go in for more tests or anything? Can you drive?" His driving has become a sore subject. In the last year, he's been in three fender benders. He keeps explaining they were accidents—as though anyone would dent a car on purpose.

"Yes, Rebecca, I spoke with Dr. Rosenberg about it." He sounds like a schoolmarm addressing kindergartners. "He says to stay off I-95 and slow down on the road."

I raise an inquiring eyebrow.

"I'm slowing down."

"I've told you before, you need to run errands, I'll take you. You could get killed driving on the highway."

He pretends he doesn't hear and calls the waitress over for the check.

As he's paying, I recall a story he told me a few years before he retired. He said he never wanted to stop working, that doing so would mean a slow and boring death. He even joked—at least I think he was joking—about putting a gun to his head if he had to let his company go. He finally retired and seems to enjoy playing cards and socializing with his neighbors. But I wonder at his wish for a sudden and violent death. Is that why he still drives? On the off chance it'll mean a fast death once he's dependent on others.

And his refusal to believe Aunt Clare's story of Grandma Yentl's close call on the Lusitania. Is it as painful to believe you might never have been born as it is to face the possibility of death?

I'm about to take a last sip of coffee when he pokes

me in the ribs and points to the floor behind the counter. A palmetto bug scurries across the tiles, then disappears as it climbs the vertical wall of the counter. My father picks up the newspaper he brought into the restaurant and rolls it into a tube. He holds it over the counter, poised for attack. When the insect climbs over the ledge and nears his plate, he raises his arm and catches my eye. I don't realize I'm holding my breath until he drops the newspaper onto the seat beside him and laughs. He throws a ten on the table and we head back to the car.

Voyage of the Damned

In May 1939, more than 900 Jewish refugees fleeing Nazi Germany boarded the SS St. Louis in Hamburg, hoping to find safe haven in Havana, Cuba. Most had applied for a visa to the United States and were planning on only staying in Cuba until able to legally enter the country. During the two weeks it took the St. Louis to cross the Atlantic, the political climate in Cuba changed and the landing permits held by those aboard the St. Louis became invalid.

After several days of negotiations, the St. Louis was forced to leave Havana. The steamship came within sight of Miami Beach's coastline as passengers awaited word on whether the United States would provide refuge. It did not. Neither the US nor any other non-European country would accept the passengers. After sailing tantalizingly close to the shores of Florida, the SS St. Louis turned east and returned to Europe.

Although the Jews were allowed to disembark in The Netherlands, Belgium, Great Britain and France, the return to Europe became a death sentence for many after Germany occupied all of these countries except Great Britain. Many were sent to concentration camps, where they perished.

A Real New York Lady

We're crossing the Julia Tuttle Causeway on one of those sparkling blue and yellow mornings that make you grateful you live in Miami. I'm driving with my windows open and the cool, fresh breeze off Biscayne Bay is whipping my hair around my face. The waves barely stir the water's surface and, as we descend from the causeway into the tightly-packed shops and restaurants of Forty-first Street, I spot clouds like thin white layers of cotton candy stretched to the point of breaking. The Schmuel Bernstein lies south of the causeway and we usually take Interstate 395. Today my father asks me to cross the Julia Tuttle to Miami Beach.

"So what's the story," I ask as I take a left off Forty-first and pull into the parking lot behind Wasserstein's Deli. "Why the detour?"

He reaches over to roll up his window, then changes his mind and sits back and shuts his eyes. "My first view of Miami Beach was across that highway."

"The Julia Tuttle?"

"It's been around a long time. The first time I saw it was during the war, when I came down here for training."

"I didn't know that. I thought you came to Miami

later with your parents."

He looks at me out of the corner of his eye, his head still resting against the seat back. "There's a lot you don't know, doll." Then he faces forward and smiles. "Like what a thrill it was to get out of the snow and ice after freezing your ass off all winter. I dreamed about it last night."

"About freezing your ass off?"

"No." He laughs and sits up. "About coming to Miami Beach for the first time. Me and my buddy, Louie, were assigned to officer's training school here and came down together from New York. We got a cab from the train station and the driver took us across the causeway to Miami Beach.

"It was unbelievable. In New York it was seventeen degrees. We stepped off the train in Florida and it was eighty. We couldn't get over it. Summer in January. The buildings, the roads, the people, everything looked brighter, more colorful—like a Technicolor Hollywood movie." He shakes his head. "I'm telling you, I was twenty and it was the first time I'd seen a palm tree. Louie too. He made the taxi driver pull over so he could climb one and pick a coconut. The *mumser*."

He's talking eagerly, obviously enjoying the memory, but suddenly stops. A strange expression crosses his face. I don't know if it's a grimace or smirk.

"What's wrong?" I ask. "You okay?"

He looks at me. I expect distress. Instead, his face takes on a wiseass sneer that means he's about to tell me something I don't need to know. I steel myself for another story about his love life.

"I ever tell you about Rita Epstein?"

"Dad, I don't need to hear—"

"Hold on there, doll. It's not what you think. Rita was a cousin. Third or fourth, I never can tell. I ran across a snapshot of her last night. She was a real New York lady."

"What's that mean?"

"You know. A sophisticated broad. Knows how to dress, how to wear makeup. A flirt."

I pull into a parking spot behind the restaurant and turn off the motor.

"Who was she?"

"You going to let me tell my story?" He rolls up the window and gets out. I follow him to the back entrance of Wasserstein's Deli and down a narrow hall stacked with milk crates. He seats himself at a booth, not bothering to inform the hostess of our arrival. He's either ignoring or unaware of the line of waiting customers who glare at us from the front of the restaurant. He calls Lena, his favorite waitress, over and places our orders for bagels and lox. I expect her to be annoyed but she greets Tootsie by name and takes it all down.

"So I told you about coming to Miami with Louie."

I nod and put the menus back in the rack near the salt and pepper shakers.

"When we got to Collins Avenue, the streets were full of soldiers. The cab driver, a nice guy, insisted on taking us to see the ocean. What a scene! It was beautiful, the sand and the water and the palm trees. And the biggest surprise of all were the rows of soldiers doing calisthenics on the beach. With their shirts off, no less. In the middle of winter!

"We dropped Louie off at the Hotel Sheldon,

where we were billeted, and I told the taxi driver to take me to The Savoy. My mother had a cousin, Stella, who moved down from New York and owned the hotel with her husband, Jack. When Stella heard I was moving to Miami, she invited me to stay with her until training began. I figured the food had to be better than what I was getting in the Army, so I agreed."

The waitress brings tall plastic glasses of ice water and he stops talking to take a sip. Then he arranges his fork, knife and spoon on top of the napkin. He looks up, confused.

"Your Aunt Stella?" I prompt him.

"Right. So the cabbie dropped me off at Jack and Stella's hotel. I was floored," he continues. "It was a classy joint. Two rows of palm trees led from Collins Avenue to the entrance, where a half dozen men smoked cigars on the front porch. Inside, the hotel sparkled, with mirrors all over the walls and blue and green tiles that Stella said were from Morocco. What really impressed me, though, were the gigantic chandeliers. At night, when they were lit, the crystals reflected off the mirrors and turned the lobby into this glittering fairy tale castle. The couches were covered in light blue silk but Stella wouldn't let me sit on them until I showered."

"It sounds like The Palms," I say, recalling a similar hotel on South Beach. "Isn't that near Fifteenth Street?"

"No. The Savoy was bulldozed years ago. Before you were born." He stops a moment to remember where he left off. "Anyway, I washed and shaved in my hotel room and returned downstairs to their apartment. Stella's husband, Jack, renovated a corner of the hotel for his family on the first floor, not far from the reception desk. Stella said I should relax, listen to the radio while she cooked. A few minutes later, my cousin, Barnie, got home. He was in high school and wouldn't shut up about joining the Navy. Then my Uncle Jack arrived. I was surprised at how tired and sickly he looked. I figured what with the war and the soldiers in the area, he was probably working too hard.

"When their daughter, Rita, came home from work, I was so floored I could barely talk. She was a looker. Shoulder-length black hair that framed a face like an angel. Lips painted the bright red girls used back then. And what a figure. The broads knew how to dress then, in high heels and sexy stockings or," he laughs, "what looked like stockings. And on top of all that, a sweetheart. A doll who did her best to make me feel at home."

I try to remember if he's mentioned the Epsteins before. I thought I knew all of our Miami relatives. Apparently not.

"So that night, a Saturday, she took me over to the Miami Beach Servicemen's Pier, where the USO set up a dance hall and rec center. The place was jumping. Hundreds of soldiers and sailors were dancing to music, talking, flirting with girls. Back then, I was quite a dancer—could jitterbug with the best. Rita could hold her own, too. Best of all though was slow dancing, holding Rita close and swaying to the music. By the end of the night, I'd fallen for her, hook, line and sinker."

"That was fast," I say. "You hardly knew her."

He smiles. "I know but it was wartime and things were different then. Everything felt more," he hesitates, "urgent. At any rate, after the dance, I walked Rita home. It was dark. Miami Beach was under a blackout order so everyone hung heavy curtains on their windows that blocked out all light and the automobile headlights and streetlights were painted halfway down. And forget about the neon lights on the fancy hotels. They were off for the duration. We were like ghosts wandering the streets.

"There was an excitement in the air, though. Thousands of young people were out and about Miami Beach, enjoying the warmth of the night and sharing this sense of purpose we all experienced after Pearl Harbor. No one talked about dying but, underneath it all, I think most soldiers shared that fear."

"Did you?" I ask. I'd never thought about Tootsie fearing death.

"Of course I did. And not just for myself. Your Uncle Moe went overseas before I did. And a lot of our friends fought in the European Theater. Most, knock wood, came home."

We stop speaking when the waitress appears with our bagels and lox. Tootsie takes a few minutes to spread his cream cheese just so, covering every centimeter of his bagel before layering on the lox and onion. When I glance toward where a line of customers wait for tables, a woman in a tennis dress scowls at me. I look away.

My father talks with his mouth full. "So I moved out of the Savoy to bunk with Louie and start my training and Rita went to her job as a waitress. But every Sunday we were together for dinner at Stella's." He takes a moment to chew and swallow. "Stella had to know something was happening between Rita and me.

Jack encouraged us. He'd slip me a five, tell me to take Rita out for a good time. Which I gladly did. It seemed like Rita and her parents did everything they could to make me fall in love with her. And I fell. Hard. Barnie never seemed comfortable though. He'd look at me funny if I slipped my arm around Rita's waist or sat too close on a sofa. I figured he was being an over-protective younger brother."

"So you and Rita were in love?"

My father sighs. "Not exactly. *I* fell in love and I thought she might be falling for me but I was too shy to ask.

"Finally, though, it was getting near the end of my training. I wanted to know where Rita and I stood. I was getting shipped overseas and wanted to find out if she'd wait for me. I had a couple days leave so I decided to spend it at my cousin's hotel. I headed over on a Friday night, looking forward to the brisket Stella made on Shabbat. After stopping, as usual, to chat with the cigar smokers on the porch, I went inside and knocked on the door to my cousin's apartment.

"The minute it opened, I knew something was wrong.

"Rita sat on the couch, crying. Stella and Jack and Barnie were there, but no one met my gaze or said hello. I walked over to Rita and asked what was wrong. She sobbed harder and Stella turned away from me. Finally, Jack led me into the kitchen and poured us each a shot of bourbon. He ordered me to sit down, then joined me at the kitchen table

"'We haven't been completely honest with you,' he said. He poured himself a second bourbon and downed it. 'You're a wonderful boy, a *mensch*.'

"I had no idea what he was talking about but waited him out.

"'We hoped you and Rita would fall in love and it would solve our problems.'

"By then I was stumped. 'What problems are you talking about?'

"'We should have told you. Rita's married.'

"I was so shocked I leaped from my chair. Jack tried to put a hand on my shoulder but I flung it off. It was all I could do to prevent myself from throwing a chair through the window. 'What the hell's wrong with you people?' I asked."

My dad's face is red and he's sweating. I hand him a paper napkin and he wipes his forehead. I try to picture Tootsie as a young man, not much older than my sons, and feel a pang of sadness for him.

"That was an terrible thing to do," I offer.

"Yeah, well Jack told me Rita married a *shegitz*." He spits out the term for a non-Jewish male. "An Italian she met at the USO. He left for the European front six months before I showed up.

"Jack said that when my mother told Stella I was coming to Miami, they hoped Rita would fall in love with me. He admitted he'd made a horrible mistake.

"I don't remember what I said. I'm sure I used some choice language. As I was talking, it dawned on me what was going on, why Rita was sobbing. I asked if her husband had died. Jack said yes.

"I didn't feel sorry for her. In fact, I was glad Rita was suffering. I felt angry and betrayed. The Epsteins lied to me and to Rita's husband. And she went along with them.

"I couldn't face Rita or Barnie after that. I was too

disgusted, too hurt. I was only twenty and felt like my life was over. I'd never trust another girl. And I sure as hell had nothing to say to Stella, who put this whole farce into action. I was shattered. I left the hotel determined never to see the Epstein family."

"So you left town without saying goodbye?"

"I didn't see Rita again. Which was fine by me. But a week later, while I was packing, Barnie showed up at my room in the Sheldon. I wasn't particularly glad to see him but I let him in.

"'Talk,' I said, not bothering to be polite.

"'I want to apologize before you leave,' he said. 'And explain.'

"'There's nothing to explain,' I told him. 'Your family handed me a line. What more is there to say?'

"'I know. I'm sorry. But you deserve to know why Rita did what she did. Why she led you along.'

"I couldn't imagine what excuse she had so I let him talk.

"'Rita eloped with Tony three weeks after she met him and my parents threatened to sit *shiva* for her, to act like she was dead. They were devastated. When he got shipped out, Rita stayed in an apartment with a few girlfriends. Neither of our parents would talk to her and she was miserable. A month after Tony left, though, Dad had a heart attack. Mom let Rita move back home to help out. When Mom learned you were coming to Miami, I guess she hoped Rita would fall in love with you and leave Tony.'

"I started to tell him I knew all this, but he held up his hand.

"'Rita went along with the plan because she blamed herself for Dad's heart attack. Maybe she also hoped she'd forget about Tony. Then, when Tony died, and you found out . . .'

"'I found out and your tramp of a sister lost a husband and a sweetheart,' I finished for him.

"He shook his head. 'I thought we were friends.'

"I opened the door so he could leave. 'Friends don't lie to each other.'"

My father drops a twenty on the table and rises. The story's made him uncomfortable and he needs to move around.

"What happened to Rita?" I ask as we return down the narrow hallway to the deli's back door.

"Who knows? I dated a couple of other girls before I met your mother, may she rest in peace. And then I was lucky enough to have you and Esther. What does it matter?"

"Aren't you even curious if she remarried?"

Tootsie shrugs. "No, I figure it was *bashert*. Fate. She would've made me miserable, a cheater like that. I never would've trusted her."

My father has never spoken with such bitterness and passion about a woman and I'm struck by the irony of his cheating on my mother after experiencing the sting of Rita's betrayal. I mention this as we walk to the car.

I expect him to be angry, but he's not. "Rebecca," he says, "if you understood that, you wouldn't be separated now. A man needs more than one woman. It's a biological fact."

I consider arguing. There's no point. My dad thinks I'm crazy for throwing Harold out after he cheated. But that's Tootsie. Driving him home, I wonder if he's still getting back at his real New York lady.

Always a View, Never a Jew

During the early 1940s, the Ku Klux Klan's national newspaper, *The Fiery Cross*, published a list of "gentiles only" hotels on Miami Beach. One of the oceanfront resorts used the slogan "always a view, never a Jew" in its advertising. Such openly anti-Semitic practices began to change in the mid-1940s when thousands of servicemen, many of them Jewish, came to the area for wartime training—then returned after the war to settle and start civilian careers.

Even after World War II, Jewish doctors could not get staff privileges in Miami Beach hospitals. In response, Jewish community leaders formed Mt. Sinai Hospital, now one of the area's biggest employers. In 1949, the City of Miami Beach banned discriminatory signs saying such things as "no pets, no kids, no Hebrew religions tolerated." Even so, no beach or golf club north of Fifth Street—an area now known as South Beach—admitted Jewish members until the 1960s.

Joan Lipinsky Cochran

Acknowledgments

I'd like to acknowledge two authors whose work proved invaluable in preparing my historical accounts. Florida International University Professor Marvin Dunn's *Black Miami in the Twentieth Century* is a thorough and fascinating study of the contributions made by African Americans to Miami's development. Raymond A. Mohl, professor of history at the University of Alabama, Birmingham, explores the relationship between Jews and blacks in Miami during the civil rights movement in *South of the South: Jewish Activists and the Civil Rights Movement in Miami, 1945-1960*. It also documents the contributions made by and includes the writings of Matilda "Bobbi" Graff and Shirley M. Zoloth, Jewish activists who provide intimate and often shocking accounts of their role in Miami's civil rights struggle.

I'd also like to acknowledge the advice and encouragement of my critique group, The Bloody Pens, particularly Prudy Taylor Board, Joe Fraracci, Buck Buchanan, Maria Amsbach, Mary Yuhas and Don

Shear. Finally, my gratitude to Deborah Shlian, M.D., and to my Master of Fine Arts thesis advisor, Dan Wakefield, and my professors, Les Standiford, Bruce Harvey, John DuFresne and Lynn Barrett at Florida International University.

About the Author

A Miami native, Joan Lipinsky Cochran lives in Boca Raton with her handsome husband, promiscuous cat and a yard full of rotting fruit. She is a freelance writer who has written for such publications as *Family Circle, the Philadelphia Inquirer, the Sun-Sentinel, The Miami Herald, the Palm Beach Post,* and *South Florida Magazine.* A graduate of Coral Gables Senior High School and Northwestern University's Medill School of Journalism, she received her masters of fine arts in creative writing from Florida International University.

You can reach Joan at
www.joanlipinskycochran.com

Made in the USA
Charleston, SC
27 March 2015